# MY FIRST BRITANNICA

# Mammals

12

ENCYCLOPÆDIA
## Britannica ®

CHICAGO    LONDON    NEW DELHI    PARIS    SEOUL    SYDNEY    TAIPEI    TOKYO

International Standard Book Number: 1-59339-048-3 (set)
International Standard Book Number: 1-59339-060-2 (volume 12)

My First Britannica:
Volume 12: Mammals 2004

Britannica.com may be accessed on the Internet at http://www.britannica.com.

# Mammals
## TABLE OF CONTENTS

**Tiger**
© Randy Wells/Corbis

## INTRODUCTION

### What kind of bears aren't really bears?
### Why are donkeys called 'beasts of burden'? What's inside a camel's hump?
### Where would you find a platypus?

In Volume 12, **Mammals,** you'll discover answers to these questions and many more. Through pictures, articles, and fun facts, you'll encounter amazing animals and learn how their habitats have changed over time.

To help you on your journey, we've provided the following signposts in *Mammals*:

■ **Subject Tabs**—The coloured box in the upper corner of each right-hand page will quickly tell you the article subject.

■ **Search Lights**—Try these mini-quizzes before and after you read the article and see how much - *and how quickly* - you can learn. You can even make this a game with a reading partner. (Answers are upside down at the bottom of one of the pages.)

■ **Did You Know?**—Check out these fun facts about the article subject. With these surprising 'factoids', you can entertain your friends, impress your teachers, and amaze your parents.

■ **Picture Captions**—Read the captions that go with the photos. They provide useful information about the article subject.

■ **Vocabulary**—New or difficult words are in **bold type**. You'll find them explained in the Glossary at the back of this volume. And there's a complete listing of all Glossary terms in the set in the ***Reference Guide and Index***, Volume 13.

■ **Learn More!**—Follow these pointers to related articles throughout the set.

And don't forget: If you're not sure where to start, where you saw something before, or where to go next, the ***Reference Guide and Index*** (Volume 13) will point the way.

### Have a great trip!

# MY FIRST BRITANNICA

# Earth's Dominant Animals

**D**espite their size differences, the great blue whale and the pygmy shrew have something in common: they are both mammals. This means that they are members of a large group of warm-blooded, air-breathing animals with backbones - and one other special characteristic. The term 'mammal' comes from the Latin word *mamma*, which means 'breast'. Every female mammal has special **glands**, called 'mammae', which produce milk. The females of all but the most **primitive** mammalian species bear their young alive. The young are then fed with milk until they have grown enough to find food for themselves.

Hair, or fur, is another typical mammalian feature. Fur keeps most mammals warm by trapping air between the strands of hair. But instead of a hairy coat, water-dwelling mammals such as dolphins and whales have a thick layer of fat to keep them warm.

SEARCH LIGHT

Mammals feed their babies
a) meat.
b) milk.
c) vegetables.

The hairy soles of this polar bear's feet protect this Arctic-dwelling mammal from the cold.
© Kennan Ward/Corbis

Mammals have existed for more than 200 million years. According to fossil evidence, they evolved from a mammal-like **reptile** group. These reptile ancestors were small active carnivores, or meat-eaters.

Two unusual groups of mammals are the marsupials and the monotremes. Marsupials have a pouch on their bellies where they carry and feed their babies. Kangaroos, wallabies, and opossums are examples

of marsupials. At one time there was even a marsupial wolf. Monotremes are egg-laying mammals. The duckbilled platypus and its cousin the echidna are the only two living examples of monotremes.

For the past 65 million years, mammals have been the **dominant** animals on Earth. This is partly because of their intelligence. Whales, seals, and dogs are among the most intelligent mammals, but monkeys, apes, and humans are the most intelligent of all.

LEARN MORE! READ THESE ARTICLES...
KANGAROOS (VOLUME 12)
PLATYPUSES (VOLUME 12)
REPTILES (VOLUME 11)

(Top) This mandrill, a colourful monkey native to Africa, is among the group of most intelligent mammals; (bottom) these dolphins are part of a group of water-dwelling mammals.

DID YOU KNOW?
The ancestors of whales and dolphins are thought to have lived on land.

# Intelligent Creatures ...Like Us!

SEARCH LIGHT

**A**pes are the most humanlike of all animals. Like people, apes do their work during the day and sleep at night. They also live in families and communities like we do. And like humans, apes sometimes fight each other. Great apes, like humans, can learn to use tools.

In the wild, some of the apes known as 'chimpanzees' use twigs and leaves as tools. They cleverly poke a twig inside the nests of ants and termites. Then they pull up the twig and eat the insects that cling to it. They make leaf cups to scoop up water. They also use leaves and twigs to clean themselves.

There are two types of ape: great apes and lesser apes. The great apes include orang-utans, gorillas, chimpanzees, and bonobos. The lesser apes include gibbons and siamangs. Apes live mostly in the tropical forests of Africa and Asia. The orang-utan, whose name means 'person of the forest', is found today only on the islands of Borneo and Sumatra.

**Why do you think that the ability to learn to make and use tools may indicate intelligence? (Hint: What do tools help you do?)**

**Family of chimpanzees.**
© Paul A. Souders/Corbis

Gibbons and orang-utans live in trees. Chimpanzees and bonobos live in trees and on the ground. Gorillas spend most of their time on the ground but sometimes sleep in trees. Most apes like to eat shoots, fruits, leaves, seeds, and grass. But while most apes will eat insects, little birds, birds' eggs, rodents, and other young animals, gorillas don't eat meat at all.

Chimpanzees and gorillas are intelligent animals. Scientists have even taught some of them to solve problems and use sign language.

Can you guess what the most noticeable physical difference between an ape and a monkey is? Apes don't have tails! And they don't have claws either. They have flat nails like we do.

LEARN MORE! READ THESE ARTICLES...
CONGO (VOLUME 8) • JANE GOODALL (VOLUME 4) • MONKEYS (VOLUME 12)

**Orang-utans, such as these from Sumatra, are among the group called the 'great apes'. Great apes are considerably more intelligent than the 'lesser apes' (gibbons).**
© Tom Brakefield/Corbis

**Answer: Tools help animals - including people - control and change their environment. Many animals have adapted to their surroundings in amazing ways. But very few besides apes and humans are able to make their surroundings adapt to them.**

## DID YOU KNOW?
A gorilla called Koko has learned some basic American Sign Language. Not everyone agrees that she is actually communicating, but most agree that she has a large sign-language vocabulary.

# Fierce but Shy Apes

**A**lthough gorillas look **ferocious**, they are actually very quiet and shy. They live in family groups in the thickest parts of jungles, where they are not likely to be disturbed. At night, the father gorillas sleep on the ground while the mother and baby gorillas sleep in big nests of sticks and leaves. Sometimes they sleep in the lower branches of trees, where they are safe from **prowling** animals.

If you were to visit a gorilla's home, the male head of the group would try to protect his family. His first step would be to beat his

**Why do you think people would make the mistake of thinking that gorillas are naturally fierce? (Hint: Look at the face of the gorilla in the large photo.)**

**Mountain gorilla family in Rwanda.**
© Yann Arthus-Bertrand/Corbis

chest, grunt, hoot, and roar to scare you away. Rather than fight you, the gorilla would hope that you left on your own.

A gorilla's feet, hands, and wrinkled face are bare and black. Its arms are so long they almost touch the ground, even when it is standing up. A gorilla's fur may be short or long, depending on where it lives. The short-haired gorilla lives in the hot, damp jungles of western Africa. The long-haired gorilla lives in the cooler high mountains of central Africa. There are not many gorillas of either kind left in the wild.

Gorillas and chimpanzees are the closest living animal 'relatives' to humans. Along with the bonobos and the orang-utans, these animals make up the 'great apes'. Like the other great apes, gorillas are very clever and can solve problems. They have good memories, and some can even learn sign language. You never know, one day you may sit down and have a chat with our cousin the gorilla!

LEARN MORE! READ THESE ARTICLES...
APES (VOLUME 12) • MONKEYS (VOLUME 12) • UGANDA (VOLUME 8)

**A male mountain gorilla like this one may weigh as much as 180 kilos. Females are smaller at up to about 90 kilos.**
© Kennan Ward/Corbis

**Answer: When we see someone with a heavy brow, we usually suppose that person is frowning and angry. People who aren't used to seeing gorillas often think that the gorillas' expressions mean they have the same feelings as people.**

## DID YOU KNOW?

Although the gibbon's thumb helps it to swing through the trees, it's a problem in other ways. The thumb is so far from the other fingers that the gibbon can't use it to control tools as a chimpanzee can.

# The Swinging Singers

SEARCH LIGHT

Why is it a useful thing for gibbons to sing?

**G**ibbons are in the family of apes, but they are 'lesser apes'. That's because they are smaller and less intelligent than great apes, such as the chimpanzee and the gorilla.

Gibbons are found in the tropical rainforests of Southeast Asia. There, the gibbon uses its long arms to swing from branch to branch in the jungle's thick **canopy**. Its long, thin hands and feet help make the gibbon a very good **aerial acrobat**. The gibbon's thumb starts at the wrist and not the palm of its hand. This means the thumb acts like a hook on branches. The gibbon's feet also have a long split between the big toe and the other toes. This split provides a firm foothold on branches.

Because they are so well suited to tree climbing, gibbons spend most of their time travelling along branches. And they don't have to leave the trees for dinner. Gibbons eat fruit, leaves, vegetables, and insects, all of which are found in the canopy.

**White-handed gibbon, also called Malayan lar.**
© Tom McHugh/Photo Researchers

Gibbons live in small family groups of a male, a female, and their young. The male and female 'sing' in the morning and evening, and the males sometimes give solo performances. Gibbons are **territorial**, and singing lets everyone know that they are at home. The moment the family home is threatened, gibbons hoot and leap and swing with great excitement.

Gibbons are a great attraction at zoos because they are such fun to watch. Unfortunately, they are in danger of disappearing altogether in the natural world.

LEARN MORE! READ THESE ARTICLES...
APES (VOLUME 12) • ASIA (VOLUME 7) • RAINFORESTS (VOLUME 1)

**The grey gibbon lives on the island of Borneo in Southeast Asia.**
© Uwe Walz/Corbis

Answer: When gibbons sing, they are letting other gibbons know where they are.

SEARCH LIGHT

Most monkeys live in
a) the Himalayas.
b) hot deserts.
c) tropical rainforests.

# Cute Clowns and Big Bullies

**V**isitors to a zoo are always attracted by the **antics** of monkeys. Many animals have tails. But none use them in as many ways as monkeys do. And no monkey uses its tail as cleverly as the spider monkey.

(Top) Family of baboons in Tanzania, Africa; (bottom) Central American spider monkey sitting on a tree branch.

The furry spider monkey is the champion **acrobat** of the monkey world. Its long arms help it to swing through trees. Its tail is thin, long, and very strong. It can reach almost all the way around a thick tree trunk. The tail holds onto the tree like a hand, although it doesn't have fingers.

Monkeys can be as small as kittens. The spider monkey is small, but the tiny playful marmoset is smaller - sometimes no larger than a mouse. Howler monkeys are quite big, about as big as a medium-sized dog. And their howl is so loud that they can be heard for miles. These monkeys **roam** through the trees in groups looking for food. Baboons are among the largest of all monkeys. They have dog-like snouts and large sharp teeth. They like to fight each other to see which is the strongest. The winner becomes the leader of the group.

Most monkeys feed mainly on fruits, flowers, and seeds. Some include insects and eggs in their diet. Baboons sometimes eat small mammals. Baboons live in the dry grasslands of Africa. And some macaques live in the Himalayas. But most monkeys live in warm places with lots of trees, such as tropical rainforests.

Monkeys often share their habitat with their close relatives the apes. And though apes are brainier, monkeys have a bonus too: they have tails and apes don't.

LEARN MORE! READ THESE ARTICLES…
MACAQUES (VOLUME 12) • A NIGERIAN FOLKTALE: THE MONKEY COURT (VOLUME 5)
RAINFORESTS (VOLUME 1)

Patas monkeys like this one live in bands in the grass and scrub regions of Central America.
© Kennan Ward/Corbis

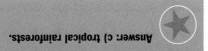
Answer: c) tropical rainforests.

**SEARCH LIGHT** ★

Why are
macaques named
after things
like crabs
(crab-eating macaque)
and lion tails
(lion-tailed macaque)?
(Hint: How do people
sometimes get their
nicknames?)

# Smart Monkeys!

The monkeys called 'macaques' are known to be very intelligent. They're also known to be bad-tempered sometimes.

Macaques are found mainly in Asia. They have arms and legs of about the same length. Their fur is usually a shade of brown or black.

**Rhesus monkey, a familiar macaque.**
© Craig Lovell/Corbis

Their **muzzles** are dog-like. The tails of each kind of macaque are different. Some are long, some are of medium length, some are short, and some are missing altogether!

Macaques also come in different sizes. The crab-eating macaque is the smallest and the Tibetan macaque is the largest. Males are larger and heavier than females. Crab-eating macaques are long-tailed monkeys with whiskery brown faces. They fish for crabs, lobsters, and shrimps. These macaques have been used in **research** to develop medicines that prevent the spread of **polio**. Lion-tailed macaques have black fur, with long grey hair around their necks and a puff of hair at the end of their tail. Their numbers are going down, and they are now found only in a small part of southern India.

Have you ever heard the saying: 'See no evil, hear no evil, speak no evil'? It comes from the Japanese Buddhist religion, and the picture of three monkeys that usually illustrates the saying is of Japanese macaques. These are large, muscular, shaggy-haired monkeys with pink faces and short furry tails.

One of the best-known macaques is the rhesus monkey. These macaques have often been used in medical experiments. The Rh factor, which is one of the traits that doctors use to identify different blood types, is named after the *rh*esus monkey.

LEARN MORE! READ THESE ARTICLES...
BUDDHISM (VOLUME 5) • MONKEYS (VOLUME 12)
A NIGERIAN FOLKTALE: THE MONKEY COURT (VOLUME 5)

**These Japanese macaques groom each other and play in Nagano. Macaques are known for their intelligence as well as their tempers.**
© Michael S. Yamashita/Corbis

**DID YOU KNOW?**
Although rhesus monkeys are still often used in medical experiments, many people are asking scientists to stop using animals this way. As a result, many scientists now plan experiments so that fewer animals are used.

**Answer:** Macaques are commonly named after features that make them different. So the crab-eating macaque was named after its diet. The lion-tailed macaque was given its name because its tail looks like that of a lion.

© Wolfgang Kaehler/Corbis

# Monkeys' Primitive Cousins

Lemurs have lived on Earth for a very long time, but they are found in only two places: Madagascar and the Comoro Islands, off the eastern coast

**Mother and baby ring-tailed lemurs.**
© Kevin Schafer/Corbis

of Africa. Millions of years ago, the island of Madagascar broke away from the continent of Africa. On the continent the monkeys were smarter than the lemurs, and the lemurs all died out. But no monkeys ever reached Madagascar, so the lemurs did well there without any competition.

The best-known **species** of lemur, the ring-tailed lemur, has a long striped tail, with rings of black and white. Like most lemurs, it lives in trees but looks for food on the ground. When walking on the ground, the ring-tailed lemur waves its tail back and forth, high in the air over its back. But lemurs don't hang from trees by their tails, as some monkeys do. Instead lemurs' tails help them keep their balance and sail through the air from tree to tree, like the ring-tailed lemur in the large photo.

Lemurs are mild, shy animals, but they can be very curious when there is food around. They have a better sense of smell than monkeys have, and they use it to find fruits, leaves, insects, and small birds to eat. Most of this activity takes place at night, because lemurs like to sleep during the day.

Lemurs usually have only one baby at a time. The baby clings to its mother's underside and travels with her through the treetops. After a while, the baby lemur rides on its mother's back.

LEARN MORE! READ THESE ARTICLES...
CHAMELEONS (VOLUME 11) • MADAGASCAR (VOLUME 8)
MONKEYS (VOLUME 12)

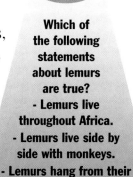

SEARCH LIGHT

**Which of the following statements about lemurs are true?**
- Lemurs live throughout Africa.
- Lemurs live side by side with monkeys.
- Lemurs hang from their tails like monkeys do.

Answer: None of these statements are true.

## DID YOU KNOW?

If you've ever been licked by a cat, then you know that cats have rough tongues. They all do. This is because their tongues are covered with little sharp-edged pockets. The pockets help them lick up water and groom their fur.

# The Tiger in Your House

**SEARCH LIGHT**

Name one thing that house cats have in common with lions? How are they different?

If a cat lives with you, you have a member of a proud, sometimes fierce family as a pet. A tiger is a cat. So are lions, leopards, and cheetahs. Jaguars, lynx, panthers, and pumas are cats too.

All cats have five toes on their front paws and four on their back paws. They have long sharp claws. They use their claws for climbing trees, catching food, and protecting themselves against other animals. All cats except the cheetah can move their claws in and out.

**Pet cat being cuddled.**
© Jose Luis Pelaez, Inc./Corbis

All cats purr, making a low, continuous, rattling hum. The purr is a relaxing, self-comforting sound that can signal a friendly mood. Many cats also meow, though 'big cats' (such as lions and tigers) roar. Most cats don't like to go in water, but they can all swim if they have to. Cats can hear even faraway things. And they can see at night when it's very dark. They are also among the fastest animals on Earth. In fact, the cheetah can run faster than any other animal, but only for a short distance.

Though **domestic** cats are usually fed by their owners, cats naturally get their food by hunting. They'll eat anything from mice to zebras, depending on how big a cat they are. Some will eat fish, clams, and snails. When house cats play with string and small toys, they're displaying their ancient family hunting **instinct**.

Cats have existed on the Earth for a very long time. The people of Egypt were the first to keep cats as pets. They gave them milk in gold saucers and made statues of cats. When cats died, they were often buried in special graveyards or even made into mummies!

LEARN MORE! READ THESE ARTICLES...
EGYPT (VOLUME 8) • OCELOTS (VOLUME 12) • TIGERS (VOLUME 12)

The domestic cat (house cat) is one of the most popular house pets. In ancient Thailand, cats lived in kings' castles.
© Craig Lovell/Corbis

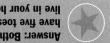

**Answer: Both lions and house cats eat meat. They also both purr, have five toes on their front feet, and are very quick. But cats can live in your house. Lions are too big and too wild to be pets.**

Most people think of tigers as hot-weather animals. But the photograph shows how well tigers have adapted to the cold. What things show you that tigers can live well in the snow?

Of the five kinds of tiger that remain, the Bengal tiger is the best known of these big cats. Here a mother Bengal tiger rests with her cubs.
© Tom Brakefield/Corbis

# The Striped Big Cats

The tiger is the largest of the big cats. Unlike other big cats, tigers have stripes all over their bodies. The size and colour of the stripes are different depending on the kind of tiger and where it is found.

The background colour can be anywhere from a light yellow on the belly to a deep yellow or orange on the back. Dark stripes cover the tiger's head, body, and legs. There are also black rings on its tail. On a domestic cat these stripes would be called 'tabby' marks.

The colouring of the tiger acts as **camouflage**, making it hard for its **prey** to see it crouching in the grass. Tigers prey on many wild animals. But they will also kill cattle, horses, sheep, and goats. If it gets very hungry, a tiger can even kill an ox. Tigers usually stay away from large animals such as elephants, buffalo, and bears. They also try to stay away from people. When they do attack people, it is usually either to save themselves or because there is a **shortage** of other

**Tigers can purr just like domestic cats. The difference is that domestic cats can keep up a constant purr, while tigers purr only when they breathe out.**

food. Sometimes an injured tiger will attack a person.

**Siberian tiger walks through the snow.**
© W. Perry Conway/Corbis

Tigers are found only in Asia. There used to be eight different kinds of tiger, but only five remain. The best known is the Bengal tiger, found mainly in India. The rare Siberian tiger is larger and has longer, softer fur. The Bengal and Siberian tigers are the ones most often seen in zoos. The other kinds of tiger are the South China, Indo-Chinese, and Sumatran. There are no more Caspian, Javan, or Bali tigers left in the world. These tigers are extinct.

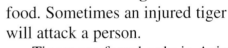

LEARN MORE! READ THESE ARTICLES…
CATS (VOLUME 12) • A KOREAN FOLKTALE: THE TIGER IN THE TRAP (VOLUME 5)
LIONS (VOLUME 12)

**Answer: First, this Siberian tiger has a thick coat of fur, great for cold weather. You may also have noticed the tiger's large feet, ideal for walking on snow. Large feet act as snowshoes and keep the tiger from sinking too far into the snow.**

# Meet the King and Queen of Beasts

**U**nlike all the other big cats, lions live in groups, called 'prides'. Prides of lions can be found on grasslands, in desert areas, and on rocky hills. But except for African animal parks, there are few places left in the world where lions still roam free. Today the only wild lions outside Africa are a few hundred protected animals in the Gir Forest National Park in north-western India.

Each pride is made up of lionesses (female lions) of different ages but all related to each other, plus their cubs, and one or two adult male lions. A pride may have as few as 4 or as many as 37 members, but about 15 is the usual number.

**Male lion.**
© Randy Wells/Corbis

SEARCH LIGHT

The male lion in the smaller photo has a big shaggy mane. Why do you think male lions have manes? (Hint: Male lions guard and protect the pride's territory.)

During the day lions lie in the shade or climb trees and rest on the branches. But they become very active at night. Like other cats, they can see well in dim light and like to hunt in the dark. Lions hunt grazing animals, such as zebras, antelopes, buffaloes, and gazelles.

Most lions will not attack a human or a large animal such as a giraffe or a hippopotamus. But lions that live near villages may carry away donkeys, goats, or even small cows. Imagine how strong a lion's teeth and neck have to be to lift a cow over a fence!

A male lion is usually identified by its big fur collar, called a 'mane', and by the dark **tuft** of hair on its tail. Females are the same sandy colour as males, but they are a little smaller. Lion cubs have dark spots when they are born.

You may think that lions only roar, but they also growl, grunt, and cough. Sometimes they even purr like giant pussycats.

LEARN MORE! READ THESE ARTICLES…
CATS (VOLUME 12) • NAMIBIA (VOLUME 8) • TIGERS (VOLUME 12)

Female lions such as these do most of the hunting. The males usually roar to 'scare up' the prey while the females lie in wait.

© Tom Brakefield/Corbis

Answer: A male lion has to look fierce and strong to scare off other animals. The mane makes him look bigger and scarier.

© Tom Brakefield/Corbis

# Spotted American Cats

**W**hen we think of cats, we usually think of small domestic cats or big cats like lions and tigers. But there are many kinds of cat of all sizes still living in the wild. One such cat is the ocelot. The ocelot is about twice the size of a domestic cat.

**Ocelot of Costa Rica, in Central America.**
© Kevin Schafer/Corbis

The ocelot is found in the Western Hemisphere, from Texas in the south-western United States down to Argentina in South America. It lives in several different habitats, including tropical forests, grasslands, and brush.

The ocelot's fur is short, smooth, and yellowish grey. There are small black spots on its head, two black stripes on each cheek, and four or five black stripes along its neck. This coat is good **camouflage** for the ocelot. It makes the animal hard to see in the leafy shade, for example. But its patterned fur is also attractive to humans. People hunt the ocelot for its fur, and so the number of ocelots in the wild has shrunk. In the United States, it's illegal to hunt ocelots or to sell their fur.

In the wild, ocelots generally like to live alone. They sleep during the day, usually in a tree or in other heavy plant cover. At night they hunt for rodents, birds, reptiles, and fish. However, they will also kill pets and other small **domestic** animals left outdoors.

Ocelot kittens start hunting with their mother when they are about three months old. When they are a year old, they leave the mother and start living on their own.

Some people try to keep ocelots as pets, since they are easily tamed when they're kittens. But when they grow up, the adult ocelots can sometimes be bad-tempered.

LEARN MORE! READ THESE ARTICLES…
CATS (VOLUME 12) • CENTRAL AMERICA (VOLUME 9)
TIGERS (VOLUME 12)

SEARCH LIGHT

**Look at the small photo. Why do you think it's hard to know just how many ocelots there are in some areas? (Hint: What do the spots on the ocelot's fur do for it?)**

**Answer:** Ocelots sleep during the day in trees and other areas with dense leaf cover. An ocelot's spotted coat helps it blend into a leafy background and makes it difficult to see, day or night.

SEARCH LIGHT

About how much difference is there between the tallest dog mentioned in the article and the shortest one mentioned?

Dogs, some of the most popular animals in the world, come in many shapes and sizes. They were among the first animals to be domesticated, or tamed, by humans.

© Tim Davis/Corbis

# The Loyal Companions

For thousands of years, dogs have held a special place in people's hearts. They are known as 'man's best friend'. This is because they are so brave, loving, and loyal. Dogs are used to living in groups called 'packs' and obeying the pack leader. Now humans are their pack leaders. Dogs depend on people for food - mostly meat - and perform services in return.

Since prehistoric times, dogs have worked for people. They have tracked game animals and retrieved them on land and water, guarded

Security guard with police dog examining bags at a convention in Mexico.
© AFP/Corbis

houses, and pulled sledges. They have delivered messages, herded sheep, and even rescued people trapped in snow. They sniff out illegal drugs and explosives, help police make arrests, and guide visually impaired people. Fast-running dogs are also used in races.

Dogs have many abilities and characteristics that make them useful. Sharp teeth are one of these. Most dogs can smell fainter odours and hear higher notes than any person. And although dogs don't see many colours, they are very good at noticing movement.

Dogs come in many shapes, sizes, and **temperaments**. A big Irish wolfhound stands about 80 centimetres high at the withers, or top of the shoulders. The chihuahua, however, stands about 13 centimetres tall. Herding dogs such as collies tend to be intelligent. Terriers, which were bred to catch rodents, were originally quite fierce. But many different breeds of dogs now make playful family pets.

Dogs have been **domesticated** for much of human history. When Pompeii - the ancient Italian city that was buried by a volcano in AD 79 - was excavated, a dog was found lying across a child. Apparently it was trying to protect the child.

LEARN MORE! READ THESE ARTICLES…
AESOP'S FABLES: ANIMAL STORIES THAT TEACH (VOLUME 5)
CATS (VOLUME 12) • WOLVES (VOLUME 12)

Answer: On average, the difference between the Irish wolfhound and the chihuahua is 69 centimetres.

29

The grey wolf is also known as the 'timber wolf'. In spite of its name, the grey wolf may be brown, reddish, black, or whitish on its back.

© Tom Brakefield/Corbis

SEARCH LIGHT

Fill in the gap: The alpha male and female are the pack _____.

# Noble Hunters, Strong Families

**W**olves are very intelligent animals. They are also quite social - living and hunting in family packs. They have a strict ranking system, with a **dominant** female and male - the alpha pair - leading the pack. Only the alpha pair mate and have puppies, though the whole pack helps raise the young. Four to seven pups are born at a time.

Packs have 7 to 30 members, depending on how much **prey** is available. Each pack patrols a home territory of 100 to more than 1,000 square kilometres. They define their territory with scent markings and with growls, barks, and their legendary howl.

**Adult grey wolves and cub.**
© Tom Brakefield/Corbis

Even though they're not terribly fast, wolves are excellent hunters. They tackle much larger animals and can even bring down huge moose and bison. Usually they hunt caribou and elk, but they might even eat mice if that's all they can find.

Wolves hunt by using their keen senses and group cooperation. They work by tiring out their prey, sometimes chasing them all night. At the end they encircle their prey, waiting for the chance to attack unexpectedly. As soon as the animal is brought down, the pack will feed. The highest-ranking members eat first and get all the tastiest bits.

Wolves belong to the canine family. Their relatives include jackals, coyotes, dingoes, New Guinea singing dogs, wild dogs of Africa, and the **domestic** dogs people keep as pets.

Scientists believe that wolves may be the original canine from which the others descended. However, only three **species** of wolves remain today. There are grey wolves in Europe, Asia, Canada, Alaska, and Yellowstone Park (U.S.). A few hundred Ethiopian wolves live in a small part of Africa. Red wolves now survive mostly in **captivity**, but they used to roam the south-eastern United States.

> ## DID YOU KNOW?
>
> Wolves have often proved helpful wherever they live. They help control the numbers of rodents and deer. And by leaving dead prey remains behind, wolves provide meals for many other animals.

LEARN MORE! READ THESE ARTICLES...
BISON (VOLUME 12) • CANADA: LAND OF LONG WINTERS (VOLUME 9)
DOGS (VOLUME 12)

**Answer: The alpha male and female are the pack leaders.**

# Howling at the Moon

Alone coyote howling at the Moon is probably familiar to anyone who's watched cowboy movies. It's true that the coyote is famous for its night concerts. Sometimes it utters short yaps and at other times it makes long howls. This is how coyotes communicate, but to people coyotes sound sad.

The coyote is mostly found in North America. It is sometimes called the 'little wolf' or 'brush wolf'. This is because it is related to the wolf. Both are members of the dog family. But the coyote is smaller than the wolf.

The coyote's fur is long and rough. It is greyish brown in colour, although there is sometimes a patch of white at the throat and belly. The **muzzle** is narrow and has a darker colour. A coyote's legs may be reddish and its tail bushy and black-tipped.

The coyote is most active after dark. It hunts for its food alone or in a group called a 'pack'. It generally feeds on **rodents** and **hares**. A coyote can follow and chase animals for long distances. Sometimes coyotes like to eat vegetables, fruit, and insects.

**Coyote roaming the forest.**
© Royalty-Free/Corbis

To find a mate, a coyote may travel for miles. The coyote pair, the male and the female, sometimes stay together for life. Both parents look after the pups. The young live with their parents for as long as three years. They help to look after and protect their brothers and sisters that are born after them.

Sometimes coyotes have been hunted and killed to protect farm animals. But they can still be found in many areas where people live.

LEARN MORE! READ THESE ARTICLES...
GRAND CANYON (VOLUME 9) • RABBITS AND HARES (VOLUME 12)
WOLVES (VOLUME 12)

SEARCH LIGHT

**Coyotes are part of which family?**
a) cat
b) dog
c) Jones

**Coyotes are well known for the various sounds they make. At times it appears that they're howling at the Moon.**
© Jeff Vanuga/Corbis

DID YOU KNOW?

Most people think of the American Wild West when they think of coyotes. But coyotes have been showing up all over the United States. Some have even been seen in New York City.

Answer: b) dog

33

SEARCH LIGHT

Why do you suppose raccoons are sometimes called 'bandits'?

# Masked Bandits

The raccoon is a smart and curious animal, easily recognized by the black mask across its eyes and the black bands ringing its bushy tail. These bands give the raccoon its nickname, 'ringtail'.

To many people in North and South America raccoons are animals that dig through rubbish during the night at campsites and in town rubbish bins. They're **nocturnal** animals, sleeping in the daytime, and they eat many different kinds of foods. Raccoons often search in shallow water for food such as frogs and crayfish, and this once caused people to believe that raccoons washed their food.

Raccoons' bodies usually measure 50 to 66 centimetres long, and their tails are about 30 centimetres long. They weigh about 10 kilos, though a large male may weigh more than twice that amount. A raccoon's **forefeet** look like slender human hands, and the creature can handle objects quickly and easily.

**A raccoon at a pond.**
© D. Robert & Lorri Franz/Corbis

Raccoons range from northern Alberta, in Canada, through most of the United States and into South America. They like wooded areas near water, but many also live in cities. They swim and climb, and they often live together high in hollow trees, in openings in rocks, in tree stumps, or in other animals' burrows. In cities they are often found living in the attics of houses.

In spring a female raccoon usually has three or four babies. When they are 10 or 11 weeks old, the mother starts taking them on short outings. The young stay with their mother for about a year.

Raccoons are considered pests in some areas, and in the eastern United States they are the primary carrier of the disease **rabies**.

LEARN MORE! READ THESE ARTICLES...
NORTH AMERICA (VOLUME 9) • PANDAS (VOLUME 12) • PORCUPINES (VOLUME 12)

**DID YOU KNOW?**
The name 'raccoon' comes from a Native American Indian word for the animal. Other names taken from Native American Indian languages include caribou, opossum, skunk, and woodchuck.

Raccoons that are used to being around people may seem so friendly and cute that you want to pick them up. Don't! They're still wild animals with sharp teeth, and they may carry diseases.
© Joe McDonald/Corbis

Answer: They are called bandits because they look like they are wearing masks and because they steal food from rubbish bins.

# Snakes' Feared Rivals

**C**urled up in its soft burrow, the shaggy-haired mongoose looks gentle and harmless. But when it's hungry, a mongoose is a very dangerous creature. Some people call the mongoose 'furred lightning' because it can move faster than a snake can strike. This makes the mongoose the most famous snake killer in the world.

There are over 40 species of mongoose living in Asia, Africa, and Europe. India is home to both the mongoose and the cobra, a highly poisonous snake. When a mongoose meets a cobra, the mongoose uses its speed and sharp teeth to grab the snake behind the head. Then it hits the cobra against the ground until the snake is dead.

**Yellow mongoose, also called meerkat.**
© Martin Harvey—Gallo Images/Corbis

Because of their snake-fighting ways, mongooses are very welcome in places where there are many poisonous snakes. Sometimes people in these places keep mongooses as pets. But mongooses aren't allowed in most countries of the world, not even to be kept in zoos. It is dangerous to bring even a few mongooses into a country where they do not naturally live.

Some countries have made the mistake of **importing** mongooses to help kill snakes and rats. The problem is that once the mongooses have killed and eaten most of the snakes and rats, they still need food. So the mongooses hunt the other small animals that they can catch, and they can catch almost anything. No bird, rabbit, or squirrel is safe from the 'terror of the fields'. Few small animals are quick enough to escape a hungry mongoose.

LEARN MORE! READ THESE ARTICLES…
INDIA (VOLUME 7) • KING COBRAS (VOLUME 11)
THUNDER AND LIGHTNING (VOLUME 1)

SEARCH LIGHT

Can you tell from the large picture how a mongoose keeps from getting bitten by snakes? (Hint: The snake's tail is still on the ground.)

This yellow mongoose in Botswana has just
won its battle with a snake.
© Gallo Images/Corbis

Answer: The mongoose grabs the snake just behind the head so
that the snake can't reach it with its fangs.

# Cuddly Exotic Bears

**W**hen you think of pandas, you probably picture a big cuddly black-and-white bear. But there are actually two kinds of panda: the giant panda and the lesser panda. The giant panda is the familiar black-and-white animal, which is found mostly in the forests of China and Tibet. The lesser panda looks rather like a raccoon.

The giant panda grows to about 1.5 metres long and 100 kilos. Its favourite food is bamboo, and it eats almost nothing else. It needs to consume large quantities of bamboo to get the nourishment that its body needs, so it spends about 10 to 12 hours a day eating. **Captive** pandas, like those found in zoos, have a broader diet. In addition to bamboo, they may eat cereals, milk, and garden vegetables.

**Lesser panda.**
© Keren Su/Corbis

The lesser panda is smaller and has rich reddish brown fur on its back and black fur on its belly. It has a bushy ringed tail that makes it look a little like a raccoon. The lesser panda is sometimes called a 'cat bear' or 'red bear cat'. It's found in China, as well as in the South Asian countries of Myanmar, Nepal, and India. Like its giant cousin, the lesser panda also eats bamboo. But it also eats grasses, fruits, other plant material, and, sometimes, small animals.

Giant pandas are endangered animals. Their natural habitat keeps shrinking each year. But many countries are trying to help China preserve its bamboo forests so that pandas have a place to live. People are also working to increase the number of pandas by breeding them in zoos.

LEARN MORE! READ THESE ARTICLES…
BAMBOO (VOLUME 10) • CHINA (VOLUME 7) • KOALAS (VOLUME 12)

There are probably only about 1,000 giant pandas left in the wild. Another 100 or so live in zoos.
© Keren Su/Corbis

SEARCH LIGHT

In the wild, giant pandas get most of their food from bamboo plants. What will happen if people in China keep cutting down the bamboo forests?

DID YOU KNOW?
Many people call the panda a 'panda bear', but for a long time scientists weren't sure if it really *was* a bear. Today, in spite of some non-bear traits, the panda is usually classified in the bear family.

Answer: If people continue to cut down the bamboo forests, then giant pandas will starve and die out. They simply couldn't adjust to a life without bamboo.

# Strong and Graceful Animal Friends

**T**he horse has been a friend to human beings for thousands of years. Long ago, horses were used to carry soldiers onto the battlefield. They have also pulled carriages, carts, and heavy farm machinery. Today people ride horses and use them for hunting, playing **polo**, and racing. Horses even perform in circuses.

**A herd of galloping horses in New Zealand.**
© Kit Houghton/Corbis

The reason horses have been used in so many ways is because they are large and strong. A typical horse weighs more than 450 kilos! It can stand more than 1.5 metres tall at the shoulder. From its nose to its tail, it's about 2.7 metres long.

The legs of a horse are strong even though they look very slender. When a horse is moving, its back legs give it the power to move forward and its front legs give it support.

A horse's foot is really just one large toe, and the hoof is like a thick toenail. The part of the hoof that can be seen when the horse's feet are on the ground is called the 'wall'. A horseshoe is fitted to the underside of the wall to protect it from cracking.

A horse's eyes are larger than those of any other land animal. But horses have a problem with sight. A horse sees things first with one eye and then with the other. So even small **stationary** objects appear to move. This frightens the horse. To keep a horse calm, the owner sometimes fits pads called 'blinders', or 'blinkers', on the outer sides of the eyes. This prevents the horse from seeing things that might frighten it.

LEARN MORE! READ THESE ARTICLES...
CAMELS (VOLUME 12) • TAPIRS (VOLUME 12)
TRANSPORTATION (VOLUME 2)

## SEARCH LIGHT

Fill in the gap:
The outside part of a horse's hoof is called the '_____'.

**DID YOU KNOW?**
Ruins of some of the world's earliest civilizations have included pictures and sculptures of horses. This proves that people have been working with horses for thousands of years.

Many people still enjoy horseback riding. This woman is riding seated in what's called a 'stock saddle'. American ranchers and cowboys developed this comfortable seat. The more formal 'English saddle' is used with many show horses.

© Royalty-Free/Corbis

Answer: The outside part of a horse's hoof is called the 'wall'.

# Beasts of Burden

SEARCH LIGHT

What's one way that donkeys are like horses? What's one way that they're different?

**D**onkeys were among the first animals to be tamed by humans. The first donkeys probably came from Asia. People ride donkeys and use them to carry heavy loads, or **burdens**. Because they are surefooted, donkeys are useful on rough or hilly ground.

Donkeys play an important part in the lives of people in the mountains of Ethiopia and other parts of northeastern Africa. They are also important to the people in the high plains of Tibet and in parts of South America.

Donkeys can be found in a range of sizes. From the ground to the shoulder, the American donkey can be 168 centimetres tall, while the Sicilian donkey is only about 81 centimetres tall. The donkey's long ears are its most noticeable feature. Donkeys are usually white, grey, or black in colour, or shades in between. Most of them have a dark stripe from their mane to their tail. The mane of a donkey is short and tends to stick out.

**Donkey carries load through the streets of Colombia, South America.**
© Jeremy Horner/Corbis

Donkeys can survive on almost any kind of plant for food, but usually they eat hay or grass. They are gentle and patient and become fond of their masters if they are treated well. This is why some people prefer donkeys to horses or mules.

The donkey is related to the horse. Sometimes people **crossbreed** a donkey with a horse. When the father is a donkey and the mother is a horse, the baby is called a 'mule'. Another name for a donkey is a burro, which is the Spanish word for the animal.

LEARN MORE! READ THESE ARTICLES...
CAMELS (VOLUME 12) • HORSES (VOLUME 12) • TRANSPORTATION (VOLUME 2)

This donkey shows how important these animals can be
to their owners. Donkeys are gentle and patient and
become fond of their masters if they are treated kindly.
© Galen Rowell/Corbis

## DID YOU KNOW?
Donkeys can be famously stubborn.
If they don't want to move, then no
amount of pushing or pulling will
budge them.

Answer: Donkeys and horses look very much alike, with similar
faces, legs, bodies, tails, and manes. Horses, however, are
generally much taller than donkeys. And donkeys are generally
considered better pack animals and are more patient than horses.

**SEARCH LIGHT**

What are three reasons that tapirs are becoming endangered?

This Malayan tapir is related to the horse, but it looks more like a pig. To add to the confusion, its baby is called a 'calf', like a cow's baby.
© Kevin Schafer/Corbis

## DID YOU KNOW?
A mother tapir carries her baby for about 13 months before it is born. That might seem like a lot to us humans, who take only nine months. But it's nothing to the elephant, which carries its baby for 24 months.

# Shy Cousins of the Horse and Rhino

The tapir is a strange-looking animal. It has a stumpy tail and a soft flexible snout like a short elephant trunk. Some tapirs are brown or grey. Others have a black head and legs, with a dirty-white back and belly. Its feet have hooves, just like a horse.

In fact, tapirs are related to horses, and to rhinos too. You wouldn't know it to look at them, since tapirs don't look much like either animal. But when it's feeding, the tapir uses its nose to move things aside and graze on plants, like a horse does.

**South American tapir of Ecuador.**
© Michael & Patricia Fogden/Corbis

The shy, **solitary** tapir is found in Myanmar, Malaysia, Thailand, and Sumatra. It also lives in the forests of Central and South America. The tapirs of Central America are the largest, about as big as a donkey.

Tapirs usually live deep in the forest near swamps and rivers. They're good swimmers and often escape from enemies into the water. In South America the tapir's main enemy is the jaguar. In Asia it has to beware of tigers.

But the tapir's greatest enemy, no matter where it lives, is people. Tapirs are endangered, which means their numbers in the wild are decreasing. This is because people cut down forests for wood and clear land to grow crops, destroying the home of the tapir and of many other animals as well. And besides the threat from tigers and jaguars, tapirs also face human hunters who kill them for food and sport.

With luck, people will soon pay more attention to preserving this unusual animal in the wild.

LEARN MORE! READ THESE ARTICLES...
CENTRAL AMERICA (VOLUME 9) • HORSES (VOLUME 12) • THAILAND (VOLUME 7)

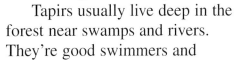

Answer: They are hunted by jaguars and tigers.
They are hunted by people.
People cut down their forest homes.

# Most Valuable Creatures on Earth

In Iran they were sacrificed to the gods. In India they are treated as **sacred**. In the ancient world they were used as money. Almost everywhere they have been used as a source of milk, butter, cheese, and meat. Cattle have, for thousands of years, been humanity's most valuable animals.

The word 'cattle' once meant all kinds of domestic animals. It comes from the Latin word *capitale*, which means 'wealth' or 'property'. The word 'cattle' is used now only for certain **bovines**, the animal group that includes oxen, bison, and buffalo.

(Top) Cows at a livestock market.
(Bottom) Longhorn resting under a tree.

A bull is a male bovine and a cow is a female - though the term 'cow' is often used for both. A calf is the young of either sex. Cattle that are between 1 and 2 years old are called 'yearlings'. The natural lifespan of cattle is about 20 years, but most of them are sent to slaughter long before they reach this age.

Today's domestic cattle in Africa, Asia, and Indonesia are very much like the cattle that lived in those areas 2,000 years ago. In Europe and America, however, cattle farmers have produced new breeds. Nowadays cattle are classified as dairy, beef, or **dual**-purpose types, which means they are used for both dairy and beef production.

One of the most popular breeds of cattle is the Brown Swiss breed. It is classified as a dairy cow in the United States and as a dual-purpose type in other countries. It may be one of the oldest breeds of cattle. A grown Brown Swiss cow weighs about 680 kilos. Other popular breeds include the Guernsey, the Jersey, and the Holstein.

**SEARCH LIGHT**

Fill in the gaps: A _____ is a male bovine and a _____ is a female.

LEARN MORE! READ THESE ARTICLES...
BISON (VOLUME 12) • ENERGY (VOLUME 2) • LOUIS PASTEUR (VOLUME 4)

Cattle have served many purposes to human beings over the years. Holstein cows such as these can be a source of dairy products.

© Gunter Marx Photography/Corbis

## DID YOU KNOW?

Cattle are ruminants - animals that bring their food back up after it has been swallowed, to be rechewed and reswallowed. This process is known as 'chewing the cud'.

Answer: A bull is a male bovine and a cow is a female.

The African or Cape buffalo are large animals with large horns. They were once hunted to the point of being endangered. Why do you think people were hunting them?

**In China, as in other parts of the world, water buffalo like this one help plough the field.**
© Vince Streano/Corbis

# Water-Loving Beasts

The American animal that most people call a buffalo is actually a bison. True buffalo live in warm places in Asia or Africa. The best known among them is the Indian buffalo. It's also called the water buffalo. That's because these animals love to lie in the water or in mud. This helps them to stay cool and keep the flies away. Buffalo eat mostly grass.

Asian water buffalo have been reared and used by people for many years. They carry loads and pull carts. Some help farmers to plough fields, especially in India and East Asia. But that's not all. Some people in Asia eat buffalo meat. They use its skin for making leather goods. Buttons, bangles and many other things are made from the buffalo's horns. And buffalo milk is rich and full of cream.

The water buffalo of Asia are heavily built and look like oxen. Some may be taller than 1.5 metres at the shoulder. The smallest buffalo are the

**Mud-caked buffalo in Kenya.**
© Yann Arthus-Bertrand/Corbis

*anoa* from Indonesia and the *tamarau* from the Philippines. They are just about 1 metre high.

All buffalo have horns, but not all buffalo horns are the same. Some curve backwards. Some curve inwards. The Asian water buffalo and the African Cape buffalo have the biggest horns. The horns of the *anoa* are short and nearly straight.

Sadly, there are very few Cape buffalo left. They were thought to be dangerous to humans and have been over-hunted.

LEARN MORE! READ THESE ARTICLES…
AFRICA (VOLUME 8) • ASIA (VOLUME 7) • BISON (VOLUME 12)

**Answer:** Cape buffalo were over-hunted for two main reasons. First, hunters enjoyed having the Cape buffalo - like other large animals - as a trophy, mainly for its large horns. Second, people were afraid of the Cape buffalo and thought it was dangerous. So, like wolves and snakes in other countries, the buffalo were often killed on sight.

# Majestic American Beasts

**Bison grazing in Wyoming's Yellowstone National Park.**
© Darrell Gulin/Corbis

The bison, or American buffalo, is the largest land animal in North America. A bull bison stands 2 metres tall at the shoulder and weighs almost a tonne. Bison once roamed the **vast** plains in herds of many thousands of animals. The shaggy bison were looking for fresh fields of tasty grass.

In order to live on the cold Great Plains, the American Indians needed rich food, warm clothing, and strong shelter. The herds of bison gave them all of these things. Bison meat was their daily food. They made warm clothes and blankets from the thick skins. They also used the skins to make **moccasins** and tents. They used the horns to make containers and the bones to make tools.

The Plains Indians killed just enough bison for their needs. The European settlers were different. With their guns they could kill bison in larger numbers than the Indians had with their arrows and spears. Some of the settlers used the bison they killed. But other people killed for sport or just to keep animals from being used by the Indians.

So there came a time when very few bison were left. Animal lovers tried to make people see how important it was to let the bison live. The governments of Canada and the United States finally put all the bison they could find into national parks and other safe places.

There probably will never be millions of bison again, but there are thousands today. There is also a European bison called the 'wisent'. The wisent is even larger than the American bison - and it is even more scarce.

### SEARCH LIGHT

The U.S. Army once killed bison to make the Plains Indians surrender. Why would killing bison achieve this? (Hint: What did the Plains Indians get from bison in addition to food?)

LEARN MORE! READ THESE ARTICLES...
AMERICAN INDIANS (VOLUME 4) • BUFFALO (VOLUME 12)
NORTH AMERICA (VOLUME 9)

**Much like the stampeding herd pictured here, the American bison once roamed the North American plains in great numbers.**
© Layne Kennedy/Corbis

DID YOU KNOW?
The bison was once so plentiful that it was used on an American coin - the 'buffalo nickel'. On the other side was the head of a Plains Indian.

Answer: The Plains Indians followed the great bison herds as they moved throughout the year. They got their food, tents, clothing, and tools from the animals. When the army killed the bison, they were killing everything the Plains Indians used for survival.

# Shaggy Beasts of Tibet

**A** yak is a heavy, strong ox with shaggy black hair and humped shoulders. Yaks and other oxen are part of the animal family that includes cattle, buffalo, antelopes, and goats. They live on the high Himalayan

**Nepalese boy leads yak.**
© Nik Wheeler/Corbis

mountain **plateaus** of Tibet (part of China), Nepal, and Bhutan. Yaks graze on grass and need a lot of water. They often eat snow in winter.

Some yaks live in the wild. But their numbers have decreased so much that soon none may be left. Bulls (male yaks) in the wild can grow as tall as 1.8 metres and may weigh twice as much as a horse. Cows (female yaks) are usually smaller and weigh less. Wild yaks live in large herds of cows, young bulls, and calves. Older bulls stay together in smaller groups.

People have also **domesticated** yaks, and these animals are plentiful. Domestic yaks are often patched black and white, and they are smaller than wild yaks. They also have longer hair than wild yaks.

In the lives of Himalayan mountain people, the domestic yak is extremely useful. People eat its meat and drink its milk. They make leather from its hide and twist its long hair into ropes and cords. Even the tail is not wasted - it is used as a flyswatter!

Because trees don't grow on the higher areas of the windy plateaus, there's very little wood available. So the yak's dried **dung** is an important fuel source to make fires for warmth and cooking. The yak is also useful for transport. Tibetans and Nepalese travel in the plateaus and mountains on the yak's back. They also use this valuable animal to carry or pull heavy loads.

LEARN MORE! READ THESE ARTICLES...
BUFFALO (VOLUME 12) • CATTLE (VOLUME 12) • NEPAL (VOLUME 7)

SEARCH LIGHT

Which of the following are ways that people use the yak?
- to provide flyswatters and rope
- to supply fuel
- for milk and meat
- to carry things and people

Like the camel and the donkey in other cultures, the
Himalayan yak is an extremely important beast of burden.
© Keren Su/Corbis

## DID YOU KNOW?
The yak also contributes to some religious ceremonies. Butter made from yak milk provides fuel for lamps used on shrines and in certain Tibetan Buddhist celebrations.

Answer: All of these things are ways people have found to make use of the yak.

Tanzania's Serengeti Plain is rich in wildlife. These male Grant's gazelles live in Serengeti National Park.
© Kevin Schafer/Corbis

# The Bouncers

**G**azelles are a graceful fast-moving antelope - part of a group that includes cattle and sheep. Gazelles live on the open plains and **semi-desert** regions of Africa. They're usually found in herds of 5 to 20 animals. Sometimes hundreds of gazelles move together, forming one large herd.

Gazelles are herbivores. That means they eat mainly herbs, bushes, and rough desert grasses. Some gazelles need more water than many plains animals. These gazelles often eat early in the morning or at night, when leaves contain more water than they do in the heat of the day.

**Thomson's gazelle in Tanzania.**
© Tom Brakefield/Corbis

SEARCH LIGHT

What are the two reasons for the decline in the number of wild gazelles?

Gazelles do one very unusual thing. As they travel in the herd, some of them bounce on all four legs. They keep their legs stiff, and as they hop, all four legs leave and touch the ground at the same time. It's not clear why they sometimes move this way. Perhaps they're just playing and having a good time. But there may be a more important reason for doing this. As they bounce in the air, the gazelles can see enemies moving toward the herd. The rest of the herd can then be warned of danger, and all can run to a safe place. And gazelles are swift runners.

Gazelle meat is a good source of food for local people. The gazelle is also food for **predators** on the plains. But the population of some kinds of gazelle is shrinking because they are often overhunted for their meat. Their **habitat** is also disappearing. Desert areas are becoming drier with fewer trees, so these areas are becoming less suitable for gazelles.

LEARN MORE! READ THESE ARTICLES…
CATTLE (VOLUME 12) • DESERTS (VOLUME 1) • NAIROBI, KENYA (VOLUME 8)

**Answer: The number of gazelles in the wild has declined because they are being hunted too much for their meat and because their natural habitat is disappearing.**

55

DID YOU KNOW?
Some breeds of horned sheep may grow more than one pair of horns. For example, Jacob sheep, a British breed that is also raised in the United States, may grow as many as three pairs of horns.

# Follow the Leader

**L**ike Mary's little lamb, sheep like to follow a leader, usually an old ram (male sheep). They live together in groups called 'flocks'. If the shepherd or farmer who takes care of the sheep can get the leader going in the right direction, the rest will follow. Sometimes well-trained and specially reared dogs called 'sheepdogs' help herd the sheep and keep them from getting lost.

(Top) Dall's sheep, a variety found in Alaska; (bottom) a boy holds a fleecy lamb (young sheep).

**Domestic** sheep are very useful animals. Their thick, soft fleece, or wool, is used for making clothes and blankets. Some sheep are raised for their meat. In many countries people drink sheep's milk, which is also used for making cheese.

A sheep's wool is cut off with **shears**, much as your hair is trimmed with scissors. Sheep are sheared only once a year, at a time when they won't be too cold without their wool. Sheep do something else that people do: they take baths. They are herded into tanks of water with chemicals in it. This mixture of chemicals and water is called a 'sheep-dip', and it is used to protect the sheep from **parasites**. Sheep also have to have shots from a **veterinarian**.

Did you know that sheep are easily scared? Even a sheet of paper blowing in the wind will frighten them. Thunderstorms also frighten them.

There are wild sheep in many parts of the world. They look a lot like goats, but there are some ways to tell the two apart. Sheep don't have beards, for example, but many goats do. Also, sheep's horns curl around the sides of their heads, but goats' horns arch toward the backs of their heads.

LEARN MORE! READ THESE ARTICLES…
AUSTRALIA (VOLUME 7) • CATTLE (VOLUME 12) • WILD GOATS (VOLUME 12)

## SEARCH LIGHT

**Which of the following is *not* a feature that sheep and goats share?**
a) giving milk
b) growing a beard
c) producing wool

Sheep are raised all over the world. This shepherd in Chile leads his sheep down a mountain road.
© Galen Rowell/Corbis

Answer: b) growing a beard

# Surefooted Mountain Climbers

**P**eople raise goats for their milk, hair, and meat. Such goats are **domesticated**. But several types of goat live in the wild - such as the ibex, the markhor, the tahr, and the goral. Domesticated goats may have descended from these wild varieties.

The ibex is a sturdy wild goat living in the mountains of Europe, Asia, and north-eastern Africa. Though ibex live in herds, old males usually live

**Mountain goats in the Rocky Mountains of Olympic National Park, Washington, U.S.**
© W. Wayne Lockwood, M.D./Corbis

alone. The European ibex has brownish grey fur. The male has a beard and large horns shaped like half circles. Other ibex include the walia and the Siberian ibex.

The markhor is a large goat once found throughout the mountains of southern and central Asia. Now only small numbers are found, and in only a few places. The markhor is about as tall as a donkey. Unlike the ibex, its horns are long and wound like a **corkscrew**. Its coat is reddish brown in summer and long, grey, and silky in winter.

The surefooted tahr lives in herds and is usually found on steep wooded mountainsides. It can be as tall as the markhor, though it often is much smaller. Three species of tahr are found from India to Arabia. The smallest is the Arabian tahr, with its short brownish grey coat. Tahr horns are short, flat, and backward curving.

The goral is found from the Himalayas to eastern Siberia. Its horns also curve backward. And like the ibex and tahr, it has a coarse coat that is brownish grey in colour. It is smaller than these other two goats, however.

LEARN MORE! READ THESE ARTICLES...
ASIA (VOLUME 7) • MOUNTAINS (VOLUME 1) • SHEEP (VOLUME 12)

SEARCH LIGHT

Which of the following wild goats have backward-curving horns?
a) ibex
b) goral
c) markhor
d) tahr

Ibex have dwindled in number in recent years. These male ibex stand in front of a glacier in their native Austria.
© K.M. Westermann/Corbis

## DID YOU KNOW?

**Mountain goats can run up nearly vertical rocks and can perch on ledges just inches wide.**

# Packed and Ready to Go

**D**id you know that a camel's hump is like a lunch box? After a good feed, a camel changes the extra food and water into fat and keeps it safe in its hump. A camel can then go for days without food or water, living on that fat. That is why people use them for crossing deserts. Camels don't have to stop all the time for a drink or a bite to eat.

When camels do get hungry, they're definitely not hard to feed. Camels eat all kinds of grass and plants, even those that are dry and thorny. In fact, a hungry camel will gobble up tents, straw baskets, and even leather belts and will drink 95 litres of water in just a few minutes!

The dromedary, or Arabian camel, has one hump. You'll find the dromedary in North Africa, the Middle East, and India. The Bactrian camel, which lives mostly in Central Asian countries, has two humps. Both camels can carry people and heavy loads. They are excellent for making long journeys. But camels can be quite bad-tempered. They bellow, bite, or kick hard if you tease them. They even spit when they're unhappy!

Camels are useful in other ways, too. Their hair is used to make tents, blankets, rugs, ropes, and clothes. Camel skin is used to make footwear and bags. Cheese and other foods are made from camel milk.

Here's an **oddity**: camels have a double set of eyelashes. These help to keep the camels' eyes safe from sand during desert sandstorms. The camel just closes its nose while long hair protects its eyes...and its ears, too.

LEARN MORE! READ THESE ARTICLES...
DESERTS (VOLUME 1) • EGYPT (VOLUME 8) • LLAMAS (VOLUME 12)

SEARCH LIGHT

True or false? Camels store extra food in their humps.

**Bactrian camel.**
© Corbis

**Dromedary, or Arabian camel.**
© Jose Fuste Raga/Corbis

## DID YOU KNOW?
If a mother camel has to go on a journey when her baby is very young, the baby is put inside a carrier on a 'nurse' camel beside the mother. If the mother can't see the baby, she'll run away, perhaps thinking her baby is lost and she needs to find it!

Answer: TRUE.

# Bounty of the Andes

The llama is closely related to the alpaca, the guanaco, and the vicuña. This group of animals is called 'lamoids'. They are part of the camel family, but lamoids do not have humps like camels.

(Top) Herding llamas in the highlands of Peru; (bottom) Quechua Indian girl with llama.

Llamas are the largest lamoids. They are about 1.2 metres tall and can weigh 113 kilos, and they have long legs and a long neck. Their coat is usually white, but some llamas are black, brown, or white with black markings.

Today most llamas are **domestic** animals. Most of them are kept by South American Indians in the mountains of Bolivia, Peru, Ecuador, Chile, and Argentina. The llama has many uses. It is a source of food and milk. It also provides wool and hair that can be used to make knitted clothing, woven fabrics, rugs, and rope. Llama **dung** can be dried and used as fuel.

The llama is also an important transport animal. It's strong, and it can go a long time without water. Also, the llama eats many kinds of plants. These traits make the llama perfectly suited for travelling over the plateaus and mountains of the Andes, where there is very little water or vegetation. A llama can carry a 45-kilo load and travel up to 32 kilometres a day!

The llama is usually gentle, but it will hiss, spit, or even kick if it is ill-treated. And a llama can be stubborn. It will refuse to work if it feels too much is being asked of it.

LEARN MORE! READ THESE ARTICLES...

ANDES (VOLUME 9) • WEAVING (VOLUME 2) • YAKS (VOLUME 12)

## DID YOU KNOW?

Llamas like to live in groups and will even live with sheep if there are no other llamas around. Shepherds often use llamas as 'watchdogs' because llamas will fight off any animal that threatens their herd.

**Which of
the following
do people get
from llamas?**
- meat
- milk
- wool
- fuel
- transportation

This llama, one of Peru's great treasures, stands in front of
a man-made Peruvian treasure, the ruins of Machu Picchu.
© Blaine Harrington III/Corbis

**Answer: Llamas provide people with all of these things.**

# Smarties
## with Dirty Faces

**D**id you know that in tests of intelligence, pigs have proved to be among the smartest of all domestic animals - even more intelligent than dogs?

The world's largest population of **domestic** pigs is in China. The second largest population of domestic pigs is in the United States, and the third largest is found in Brazil.

Besides domestic pigs, there are several species of wild pigs found in Europe, Asia, and Africa. The **pygmy** hog is the smallest of the wild pigs.

(Top) Pigs enjoying a mud bath; (bottom) getting friendly with a piglet.

It is found in Nepal and northern India. It is now in danger of becoming extinct. The warty pig and the bearded pig live in parts of Southeast Asia, Malaysia, and the Philippines.

Wild pigs eat a wide variety of foods, including leaves, roots, fruit, and reptiles. Food for domestic pigs includes maize and other grains, and some kinds of rubbish too. A pig's snout ends in a flat rounded disk. Pigs use their snouts to search for food. Both male and female wild pigs have **tusks** on their snouts, which they use for defence.

A female pig is old enough to have piglets when she is about a year old. Before she gives birth to her first **litter**, the female pig is known as a 'gilt'. After the first litter, she is known as a 'sow'. Sows can have as many as 20 piglets in a litter, but a litter of 10 or 11 is the average. A male pig is called a 'boar'. A young **weaned** pig of either sex is called a 'shoat'.

LEARN MORE! READ THESE ARTICLES...
CHINA (VOLUME 7) • TAPIRS (VOLUME 12)
WILD GOATS (VOLUME 12)

DID YOU KNOW?
People think pigs are dirty animals because they so often see pigs wallowing in mud. But pigs cover themselves with mud to stay cool. Given a choice, pigs prefer air-conditioning to mud baths.

**SEARCH LIGHT**

Find and correct the mistake in the following sentence: Pigs have proved to be among the least smart of all domestic animals.

Female pigs can have as many as 20 piglets in a litter. China holds the record for having the largest population of domestic pigs. The United States is second.

Answer: Pigs have proved to be among the smartest of all domestic animals.

# Kings of the River

**U**nderneath the water in the rivers of Africa, a giant animal moves along the muddy bottom and eats water plants. It's named after a horse, looks something like a pig, and is larger than a crocodile. It's the king of the river, the hippopotamus. Its name is a combination of two Greek words that join together to mean 'river horse'.

An African folktale describes how God created the hippopotamus and told it to cut grass for the other animals. When the hippo discovered how hot Africa was, it asked God if it could stay in the water during the day and

(Top) A herd of hippos in Botswana; (bottom) fully submerged hippopotamus.

cut grass at night when it was cool. God agreed. However, he was worried that the hippo might eat the river's fish. The hippo, however, ate only plants. At night, hippos still go ashore and wander in herds, eating grass.

Hippos have barrel-shaped bodies, short legs, and four toes on each foot. Adult hippos can weigh more than 2,700 kilos. The biggest hippos may reach 4.6 metres in length and stand 1.5 metres tall at the shoulder. Although the hippo looks clumsy on land, it is well equipped for life in the water. It swims easily, and when it stays underwater, little flaps of skin close its **nostrils**.

When a hippo is mostly **submerged**, the only things you can see are its rounded eyes, tiny ears, and raised nostrils. Sometimes a hippo lifts its head out of the water and roars. When that happens, you can see its enormous red mouth and very long teeth.

Because of the hippo's great size, its only enemies are lions and people.

LEARN MORE! READ THESE ARTICLES...
AFRICA (VOLUME 8) • ALLIGATORS AND CROCODILES (VOLUME 11)
HORSES (VOLUME 12)

## SEARCH LIGHT

Find and correct the mistake in the following sentence: When a hippo goes underwater, it constantly blows water out of its nostrils.

This hippopotamus is visiting its favourite watering hole at its African home. Hippos spend a great deal of their time in the water.
© Papilio/Corbis

### DID YOU KNOW?
Baby hippos are born in the water and can swim before they can walk.

**Answer: When a hippo goes underwater, little flaps of skin close its nostrils.**

67

**Muskrats look like a cross between a rat and a beaver. They live in water where they build a home of mud and plants that rises above the water's surface.**
© Scott Nielsen/Bruce Coleman

# The Town Builders

**M**uskrats are ratlike rodents that look a little like small beavers and live in water. The animal gets its name from the two musk **glands** under its tail. The glands give off a heavy, musky smell. Muskrats were originally found only in North America. People took them to Europe and Asia about 100 years ago, and they soon made themselves at home in those regions as well.

Muskrats build their houses in water, as a part of a 'town'. Mounds of mud, bulrushes, and other plants are heaped up into a dome-shaped structure. This rises above the surface of the water. The animals dig tunnels from under the water up into the mound. They then hollow out a room at the top, a few inches above the waterline.

Muskrats also dig narrow **channels** through the surrounding plant growth. The channels connect to each other and to other mounds. Muskrats can sometimes be seen swimming along these channels. They feed on different kinds of **sedges**, reeds, and roots of water plants, as well as **mussels**, crayfish, salamanders, and fish.

Muskrats have small eyes and ears and a long scaly flat tail. They use the tail as a **rudder** for steering or changing direction while swimming. The hind feet are partially webbed and are used as paddles.

Muskrat fur is waterproof and keeps the animals warm. Muskrats continue to be trapped because of the quality of that fur. Because of that, there are far fewer muskrats today than there were in the past.

LEARN MORE! READ THESE ARTICLES...
MOLLUSCS (VOLUME 11) • NORTH AMERICA (VOLUME 9)
PLATYPUSES (VOLUME 12)

SEARCH LIGHT

Are muskrats herbivores (plant eaters) or carnivores (meat eaters)?

# Touch Me Nots

The porcupine's name comes from words meaning 'pig' and 'spines'. This small rodent's body is covered with dark fur and the sharp quills, or spines, that give it its name. Some porcupine quills are attached in bunches, and others are attached singly. But all quills are used to protect against enemies.

**Baby New World porcupine.**
© D. Robert & Lorri Franz/Corbis

Porcupines can't actually shoot their quills through the air. When it's threatened, a porcupine puffs out its quills. The quills easily come loose if touched and stick in an enemy's skin. They can cause painful wounds and may kill if they make their way into vital organs or cause infection.

There are 25 **species** of porcupine, divided into Old World and New World porcupines.

Old World porcupines include the **crested** porcupines of Africa, Asia, and Europe. Long-tailed porcupines are also found in Asia. Brush-tailed porcupines are found in Asia and Africa.

The best-known New World species is the forest-dwelling North American porcupine. Other species found in the tropical forests from Mexico to South America use their long tails to grab onto branches. Porcupines shelter in tree branches and roots, hollow logs, burrows, and caves. Old World species like to stay on the ground more than New World porcupines do.

Porcupines are most active at night. They eat almost any tree part they can reach, including the bark. North American porcupines prefer a tender layer beneath the bark. In trying to get at it, they may chew away the bark in a ring, which kills the tree. Porcupines sometimes gnaw antlers and wooden tools such as axe handles and canoe paddles for the salt and oil they contain.

LEARN MORE! READ THESE ARTICLES…
ARMADILLOS (VOLUME 12) • MUSKRATS (VOLUME 12)
SOUTH AMERICA (VOLUME 9)

SEARCH LIGHT

Why do you think an axe handle would have salt in it that a porcupine would want?

## DID YOU KNOW?
Baby porcupines have very soft quills when they're born, kind of like cooked spaghetti. The quills stiffen quickly after the baby is born.

Old World porcupines like this one have quills embedded in clusters. New World porcupines have quills interspersed with hair, underfur, and bristles.
© Vittoriano Rastelli/Corbis

Answer: People sweat through their hands when they work. An axe handle would soak up the sweat as well as the salt in the sweat.

The slow-moving manatee lives in warm shallow coastal waters. Because manatees can't see very well, they are often injured by motorboats in their feeding areas.
© Douglas Faulkner/Corbis

# Mermaids of Yore?

SEARCH LIGHT

Stories about mermaids tell of creatures that have the head and body of a human and the tail of a fish. These stories may have come from people who saw manatees swimming and didn't know what they were.

A manatee is a large stoutly built animal with a **tapered** body that ends in a flat rounded tail. Adults grow to about 3 metres long and 360-545 kilos. The manatee has a thick tough skin and is nearly hairless. It uses its flippers for turning, holding food, moving along the bottom of rivers, and holding its young.

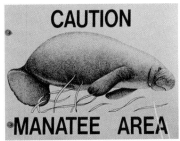

CAUTION
MANATEE AREA

Boater's warning sign.
© Catherine Karnow/Corbis

**Mother manatees and their calves communicate through**
a) chirps, grunts, and squeaks.
b) snaps, crackles, and pops.
c) dings, rattles, and creaks.

Manatees, especially the mothers and their calves, talk to each other using chirps, grunts, and squeaks. The other members of a group communicate by touching **muzzle** to muzzle. Manatees may live alone or in groups of 15 to 20.

They live in shallow waters along the coasts of oceans or in rivers that are rich in the plants they eat. The Caribbean manatee lives from the coasts of the southeastern United States to those of northern South America. The Amazonian manatee, as you might guess, lives in the Amazon River and other nearby freshwater. And the African manatee is found in the coastal waters and slow-moving rivers of tropical West Africa.

Manatees have small eyes and can't see very well. They don't move very fast either. Since manatees can't **tolerate** cool temperatures, they live in warm waters - places where lots of people like to live as well. Many manatees have been killed or injured when people drive their motorboats into the manatees' feeding areas. The manatees can't see the boats and don't move fast enough to get out of their way.

LEARN MORE! READ THESE ARTICLES...
ELEPHANTS (VOLUME 12)
MYTHS AND LEGENDS, FOLKTALES AND FABLES (VOLUME 5)
WHALES (VOLUME 12)

DID YOU KNOW?
The scientific name for the walrus,
*Odobenus rosmarus*, translates into
English as 'tooth-walking sea horse'.

# The Whale Horses

**I**n the cold Arctic seas of Europe, Asia, and North America, there lives a large creature called the 'walrus'. Its name is an English version of the **Scandinavian** word *hvalros*, meaning 'whale horse'.

The walrus has a stocky body topped by a rounded head. It has small eyes like those of a pig and a short broad mouth. Its mouth is covered with stiff whiskers. Every year, the walrus grows a new set of whiskers. An adult walrus can grow to twice the length of a Ping-Pong table.

**Group of walruses gathered on rocks.**
© Wolfgang Kaehler/Corbis

All walruses have long **tusks** growing on each side of the mouth. The tusks are very handy. The walrus uses them to fight, cut holes in ice, and pull itself out of water. Walruses spend nearly their whole life at sea. However, they often climb onto ice or rocky islands to rest and to have babies.

The walrus has flippers. In the water the flippers help the animal swim. On land the walrus uses them to walk. The walrus also uses its flippers to hold prey such as fish, but clams are its favourite food. Sometimes the animal feeds on young seals, though this happens only when it fails to find other food.

Walruses are social animals and live in groups of more than 100 members. There are two types of walrus, named for the two major oceans where they live: the Pacific walrus and the Atlantic walrus. The Pacific walrus is heavier and has longer tusks than the Atlantic walrus.

In the late 20th century, efforts were made to protect walruses. This helped increase the population of the Pacific walrus.

LEARN MORE! READ THESE ARTICLES...
MAMMALS (VOLUME 12) • NORTH AMERICA (VOLUME 9) • PACIFIC OCEAN (VOLUME 1)

**Walruses are known for their long tusks. They use their flippers to help them walk on land.**
© W. Perry Conway/Corbis

Answer: All walruses have tusks growing from the sides of their mouths that help them fight, cut holes in the ice, and drag themselves out of the water.

# The Biggest Animals of All

**W**hales live in the water. They look like fish. They swim like fish. But they aren't fish at all. Whales are 'aquatic mammals'. 'Aquatic' means they live in water. Mammals are warm-blooded creatures that give birth to live young ones and feed them with milk.

Whales can't stay under the water all the time as fish do. They have to come up for air from time to time. They breathe through blowholes at the top of their heads. When their warm breath hits the colder air outside, it makes a cloud of mist called the whale's 'spout'. You can spot a whale by its spout.

Fish can't make sounds. But whales can make two kinds of sounds. The first sounds like a bark, or a whistle, or sometimes a scream. Whales make these sounds to speak to each other. Some whales also make very loud, low sounds that other whales can hear from many miles away. This sound can be heard only under water.

The biggest whale of all is the blue whale. It can be 34 metres long and weigh around 152 tonnes. That's more than ten buses put together! Even a baby blue whale is huge.

(Top) Killer whale; (bottom) beluga whales.

Finding food is a simple matter for blue whales. They just swim along with their huge mouths open, and thousands of tiny sea creatures flow in. But blue whales have no teeth. Instead, they have strings of hardened skin, like our fingernails, that hang from the roof of the mouth. This hardened skin is called '**baleen**' and is used as a strainer to let out the water while holding back the sea creatures captured in the whale's mouth.

LEARN MORE! READ THESE ARTICLES...
FISH (VOLUME 11) • MAMMALS (VOLUME 12) • PENGUINS (VOLUME 11)

**SEARCH LIGHT**

Why do you suppose that some whales' sounds can be heard only under water? (Hint: Who's listening?)

**This humpback whale sails above the water as it grabs a breath of air. This act is called 'breaching'.**
© Brandon D. Cole/Corbis

DID YOU KNOW?
Some whales leave the water and park themselves on a beach. They may stay there so long that they die. Strangely, other whales often join the 'beached' whale - possibly to keep the first one company, according to some researchers.

Answer: Whales 'talk' to other whales, so it makes sense that their sounds would be heard where the whales spend most of their time - under the water.

# Australia's Amazing Leapers

**T**he kangaroo and its relatives are called marsupials. The mother animals among most marsupials have a pouch, or pocket, attached to their bellies. The pouch is part of their furry skin. It's where the babies stay while they are nursing. Most marsupials are found in Australia and on nearby islands.

When a kangaroo is born, it's about as long as your little finger. While it's growing, it stays safe and well fed in its mother's pouch. A baby kangaroo is called a 'joey'.

**Kangaroos visiting a golf tournament.**
© AFP/Corbis

As you can see from the large photo, when the joey is big enough, it can poke its head out of the pouch. It can then eat leaves that are close enough to reach without climbing out. As it grows bigger, it can slip out of the pouch to nibble grass. Then it climbs back into the pouch at night or whenever it is tired of hopping. If there is danger while the joey is out of the pouch, the mother kangaroo picks up her baby, stuffs it into the pouch, and hops away.

Except for the small rat kangaroo and tree kangaroo, kangaroos have extremely strong back legs. The strong legs help it make the giant leaps it is known for. Its long tail helps it keep its balance while the legs are in the air. Kangaroos are herbivores, which means they eat only plants.

Kangaroos are usually gentle and timid. But if they are cornered, they'll stamp their hind feet and growl. They can grab an enemy with their front paws and kick it with their powerful back feet.

LEARN MORE! READ THESE ARTICLES…
AUSTRALIA (VOLUME 7)
AN AUSTRALIAN TALE: HOW KANGAROO GOT HIS TAIL (VOLUME 5)
KOALAS (VOLUME 12)

SEARCH LIGHT

Find and correct the mistake in the following sentence: Kangaroos use their tails to fight.

Answer: Kangaroos use their back feet to fight.

SEARCH LIGHT

Fill in
the gap:
Koalas are
marsupials.
This means the
mothers feed and
carry their babies
in a _____
on their bellies.

# The Bears That Aren't Really Bears

**T**his roly-poly little animal has shiny black eyes that look like wet liquorice. Its funny black nose is pressed against its face between bushy grey ears. If you found this animal in your bedroom, you might think it was a toy teddy.

But this is a real animal (though it isn't a real bear), and it's called the koala. It is found only in Australia. The koala drinks dew and eats nothing but leaves of the eucalyptus tree, as shown in the large photo. It is famously slow-moving and gentle, and it sleeps up to 16 hours a day. Even when they're being **aggressive**, koalas rarely use their energy to fight. Instead they'll make loud croaking sounds known as 'bellowing'.

Koalas are related to kangaroos. Both are marsupials. Marsupial mothers carry and feed their young in a pouch on their bellies. It's like a built-in baby sling.

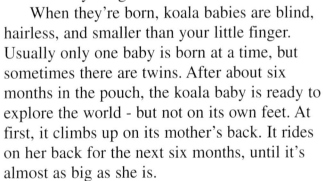

**Mother koala carrying baby on her back.**
© David and Eric Hosking/Corbis

When they're born, koala babies are blind, hairless, and smaller than your little finger. Usually only one baby is born at a time, but sometimes there are twins. After about six months in the pouch, the koala baby is ready to explore the world - but not on its own feet. At first, it climbs up on its mother's back. It rides on her back for the next six months, until it's almost as big as she is.

Mothers and babies communicate with gentle squeaks, clicks, and hums. A grunt indicates irritation or impatience. After a year the young koala leaves its mother to make its own home. Koalas are very **territorial**, and the young are not encouraged to stay once they can take care of themselves.

> **DID YOU KNOW?**
> Koalas are often slow-moving and quiet. Some people believe that their eucalyptus diet has a calming effect on them. The truth is, however, that their digestion rate is slowed down because the leaves take a lot of energy to digest.

Learn More! Read these articles...
Australia (volume 7) • Eucalyptus (volume 10) • Pandas (volume 12)

Answer: Koalas are marsupials. This means the mothers feed and carry their babies in a pouch on their bellies.

81

How many babies can a mother opossum carry in her pouch at one time?

DID YOU KNOW?
People often picture opossums hanging from tree branches by their tails. Although they wrap them around branches to help keep their balance, opossums don't actually hang by their tails.

# Playing Dead to Stay Alive

An opossum is a grey creature about the size of a domestic cat. It has a long, pointy white face and beady little eyes. The opossum sleeps in the daytime and comes out at night.

Opossums are marsupials, which are mammals that carry their young in pouches on their bellies. Like kittens and puppies, baby opossums are born blind. So the first thing they do is snuggle inside their mother's built-in belly pouch. About 13 baby opossums can fit and feed inside the pouch at one time. They stay in there and go everywhere with the mother.

**An opossum 'playing possum'.**
© Joe McDonald/Corbis

While they're in the pouch, the tiny opossums grow until they are the size of little mice. Then, after five weeks, they crawl out and ride piggyback on the mother's back. They hold on to her thick silvery-black fur with special grabbing thumbs.

Loaded with babies on her back, as the large photo shows, the mother opossum scampers through the woods and scurries up trees. She scrambles through bushes looking for fruits and berries. She climbs trees to find insects, birds' eggs, and little creatures to eat. When one of the babies gets tired, it just tumbles back into the pouch for a rest.

Opossums - or 'possums', as they're sometimes called - have another strange behaviour. Most **predatory** animals like to eat live food and will lose interest in animals that are already dead. So the opossum sometimes escapes its enemies by pretending to be dead. It will freeze like a statue and then topple over to the ground. When the predator loses interest and leaves, the opossum calmly gets up and walks away. This clever trick has become known as 'playing possum'.

LEARN MORE! READ THESE ARTICLES…
A CHEROKEE STORY: WHY POSSUM'S TAIL IS BARE (VOLUME 5)
KOALAS (VOLUME 12) • NORTH AMERICA (VOLUME 9)

Answer: A female opossum can carry about 13 babies in her pouch at one time.

# Egg-Laying Mammals

**I**f someone asked you to describe a mammal, you might say a mammal is a warm-blooded animal with hair or fur. You'd add that mammals give birth to live babies instead of laying eggs and that they feed their young with milk.

Well, the platypus feeds its babies milk. And the platypus is warm-blooded and has brown fur. But the platypus breaks a big mammal rule - it lays eggs. Platypuses and Australian spiny anteaters are the only members of an egg-laying mammal group called 'monotremes'.

Platypuses are found in the lakes and streams of Tasmania and of eastern and southern Australia. They spend their lives feeding along the bottoms of rivers, streams, and lakes and resting in burrows dug into banks.

A platypus has a big appetite. The amount of food it eats every day is almost equal to its own weight. A platypus meal may consist of insects, worms, shellfish, fish, frogs, **molluscs**, tadpoles, or earthworms.

The platypus often looks for food underwater. But in the water, the platypus's eyes and ears are closed. Since it can't see or hear underwater, the platypus depends entirely on its snout to find its food. But what a snout! A platypus snout looks like a duck's bill, which is why the platypus is sometimes called the 'duckbill'.

The platypus also has webbed feet like a duck and a tail like a beaver. When you look at it, the platypus doesn't seem to be a single animal but rather several different animals put together.

LEARN MORE! READ THESE ARTICLES...
AUSTRALIA (VOLUME 7) • BIRDS (VOLUME 11) • RIVERS (VOLUME 1)

## DID YOU KNOW?

The official name of the spiny anteater, the only other monotreme besides the platypus, is 'echidna'.

## SEARCH LIGHT

Which of the following statements about the platypus are true?
- It has fur.
- It is warm-blooded.
- It gives birth to live babies.

The platypus, so awkward and peculiar on the ground, is perfectly adapted for underwater hunting.
© Joe McDonald/Corbis

## DID YOU KNOW?
The common nine-banded armadillo is used in studies of the disease leprosy. Armadillos are some of the only animals besides humans that get the disease. And the organism that causes leprosy can't be grown in laboratories.

# The Armoured Animals

**C**an you imagine an animal covered in armour from head to toe, like a **medieval** knight? Meet the armadillo. The word 'armadillo' means 'little armoured one' in Spanish.

Armadillos are round creatures with short legs. They are about the size of a small dog. They have strong curved claws, and yes, their bodies are covered with armour. This armour is made of hard plates or scales

**Armadillo of the Andes Mountains in South America.**
© Galen Rowell/Corbis

connected by bands that stretch. If they didn't stretch, the armadillo would have great difficulty moving around.

The armour helps protect the armadillo from its enemies. But its main job is to protect the armadillo from being cut and scratched by thorns and cactuses that grow where it lives.

Central and South America are home to many kinds of armadillo. There you'll find the pichi armadillo, Burmeister's armadillo, and the pink fairy armadillo. You'll also find the giant armadillo, which is nearly 1.5 metres long. One **species**, the nine-banded armadillo, is found in Texas and several other U.S. states.

Armadillos can't see very well and are almost toothless. They hunt mostly at night and eat insects and worms, soft roots and fruits, and occasionally dead animals.

When enemies appear, the armadillo usually runs away into the tough undergrowth, where its **predators** can't follow. Sometimes the armadillo will jump straight into the air to scare its enemies. As a last resort it will roll itself up into a hard ball.

You may not believe it, but armadillos are very good swimmers. They stay afloat by swallowing a lot of air. In fact, under all that armour, armadillos are full of surprises!

LEARN MORE! READ THESE ARTICLES…
PARAGUAY (VOLUME 9) • PORCUPINES (VOLUME 12)
SOUTH AMERICA (VOLUME 9)

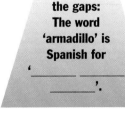

SEARCH LIGHT

**Fill in the gaps: The word 'armadillo' is Spanish for '_____ _____ _____'.**

**The long-nosed armadillo is one of South America's many varieties.**
© Martin Harvey–Gallo Images/Corbis

**Answer: The word 'armadillo' is Spanish for 'little armoured one'.**

DID YOU KNOW?
There's a bridge in Austin, Texas, U.S., that provides a roosting place for Mexican bats. More than a million at a time make this bridge their home.

# Fliers by Night

**B**ats are mammals, and like all mammals they have fur, give birth to live young, and produce milk for their young. But bats are also the only **mammals** that really fly.

Bats live all over the world, but they prefer warm climates. They like to live in huge groups, or colonies, sometimes with 1,000 bats or more in a colony. Bats sleep in caves, hollows in trees, and empty buildings.

**True or false? Bats are solitary animals.**

© Joe McDonald/Corbis

There are many kinds of bats, in many sizes. The flying fox bat, when it stretches its wings, is wider than you are tall. But the tiny Philippine bamboo bat's wings are barely 15 centimetres from tip to tip.

Most bats eat insects. The Mexican bats of Texas can eat millions and millions of insects every year! Other bats eat fruit, honey, and **pollen**. But whatever they eat, all bats look for their food at night.

© Wolfgang Kaehler/Corbis

You may have heard the term 'blind as a bat'. Bats actually see very clearly, but they don't rely on their eyes. When a bat flies, it makes sounds that we can't hear. These sounds bounce off objects in the bat's path, creating echoes which the bat's large ears can hear. The echoes tell the bat what lies ahead and help it locate food and enemies.

**(Top) Leaf-nosed bat; (bottom) fruit bat.**

Some people fear bats, but in fact they are very helpful. Not only do they eat insects that pester us, but bats also help **pollinate** many flowers and plants. Without bats, many plants, especially some kinds of cactus, wouldn't be alive.

LEARN MORE! READ THESE ARTICLES…
BIRDS (VOLUME 11) • CAVES (VOLUME 1) • ECHOES (VOLUME 1)

**Answer: FALSE. Bats live in huge groups, or colonies.**

SEARCH LIGHT

An African elephant can weigh as much as
a) a whale.
b) a bus.
c) a big snail.

# The Largest Animals on Land

**C**an you tell the difference between an African elephant and an Indian elephant?

First look at the ears: African elephants have much larger ears than

(Top) In Kerala state in India, elephants are respected and honoured. During festivals like this, they are dressed in gold faceplates that look like armour. (Bottom) Adult and young African elephants.

Indian elephants. African elephants are altogether larger and stronger and have thicker skin than their Indian cousins. In fact, African elephants are the largest animals on land. They can grow to more than 3.4 metres tall and weigh more than 5,400 kilos!

Indian elephants, found in South and Southeast Asia, are smaller, gentler, and easier to train. Most elephants in zoos and circuses are Indian. Elephants and people have long worked together. Usually, one man trains one elephant. In India, the trainer is called a *mahout*. In Myanmar (Burma), he's called an *oozie*. Both African and Indian elephants have been used in wartime.

Both kinds of elephants eat fruits, nuts, grass, and vegetables, but trees are their favourite food. To get to the best tree leaves, elephants break off branches with their trunks or sometimes just knock the whole tree down. Elephants also breathe, smell, and trumpet through their trunks. When they're hot, elephants have a bath to cool off. They swim underwater and stick their trunks up in the air so they can breathe. Elephants also have showers, using their trunks to suck up water and spray it on themselves.

Male elephants have huge tusks for digging, carrying things, and sometimes fighting. But their tusks also cause elephants problems. Hunters have killed so many elephants for the ivory in their tusks that there are not many elephants left.

LEARN MORE! READ THESE ARTICLES…
CAMELS (VOLUME 12) • KENYA (VOLUME 8) • THAILAND (VOLUME 7)

Indian elephants in Sri Lanka.
© Lindsay Hebberd/Corbis

Answer: b) a bus.

## DID YOU KNOW?
Rabbits that live in hot areas usually have bigger ears than those that live in cold areas. Larger ears help animals stay cool, while smaller ears help animals keep from getting too cold.

# Long Ears
## and Strong Legs

**I**f you see an animal outside that hops and has long ears, it could be a rabbit or a hare. Rabbits have tails that are white on the bottom. That's why some American rabbits are called 'cottontails'. Hares have longer ears and longer legs than rabbits.

**Cute and cuddly pet rabbit.**
© Kelly-Mooney Photography/Corbis

European rabbits are the ancestors of all **domestic** rabbits worldwide. Rabbits live together in underground **burrows** called 'warrens'. Inside the warren a mother rabbit carefully shreds leaves and collects grass to line a nest for her babies. Then she pulls bits of fur from her thick coat to make a warm and snug bed. Baby rabbits haven't any fur at first, so the mother must keep them warm.

The nest is usually deep enough in the warren to keep the babies safe. But when a rabbit sees a **predator** looking for the nest, the rabbit will thump its back legs to warn other rabbits. Rabbit mothers aren't gentle when their babies are in danger from dogs, foxes, snakes, owls, or hawks. They bite and kick hard with their feet!

Hares don't build warrens. Their homes are shallow holes that they dig in the grass, under trees, or in brush heaps. Some hares in cold climates have a white coat during the winter and a brown one in the summer.

Both rabbits and hares love to eat green plants such as clover as well as the bark, buds, and berries of trees and shrubs. They search for food from sundown to dawn and then hide during the day. And if you've heard the story about a rabbit jumping into a thorny bush to stay safe - it's true. Rabbits make twisting paths through thorny underbrush, where their enemies can't follow.

SEARCH LIGHT

**Fill in the gap: Rabbits have a tail that is _____ on the bottom.**

LEARN MORE! READ THESE ARTICLES...
COTTON (VOLUME 10) • KANGAROOS (VOLUME 12)
A MAYAN STORY: RABBIT THROWS AWAY HIS SANDAL (VOLUME 5)

**The American black-tailed jackrabbit is actually a hare. It's easily recognized by its long ears tipped with black colouring.**
© Darrell Gulin/Corbis

**Answer: Rabbits have a tail that is white on the bottom.**

# G L O S S A R Y

**acrobat** performer who does tricks and physical routines that require strength, balance, and body control, often above the ground

**aerial acrobat** performer who does tricks and feats above the ground or in the air, especially on a trapeze

**aggressive** openly hostile or tending to approach with great force or energy

**antics** playful or funny actions

**baleen** a hardened substance from 0.6 to 3.6 metres long found in two rows along the upper jaws of certain whales

**bovine** animal group that includes cattle, oxen, bison, and buffalo

**burden** weight or load to carry

**burrow** deep hole or tunnel made in the ground by an animal for shelter

**camouflage** colours and patterns that allow a person, animal, or thing to blend in with its surroundings

**canopy** overhead covering

**captive** (noun: captivity) taken and held in a cage or as a prisoner

**channel** narrow passageway between two areas of water

**corkscrew** device with a handle and a spiral-twist metal piece, used for removing certain bottle stoppers

**crest** (adjective: crested) standing clump of fur or feathers, usually on an animal's head

**crossbreed** to produce offspring from parents of two varieties or species

**domestic** (verb: domesticate) tame

**dominant** having influence or control over another person, place, or thing

**dual** two

**dung** animal waste

**ferocious** fierce and wild

**forefoot** one of the front feet of an animal with four or more feet

**gland** structure in animals that produces special substances, such as sweat or saliva or milk

**habitat** the physical environment in which a living thing dwells

**hare** rabbit-like animal

**import** to bring from a foreign place

**instinct** natural tendency of a living thing to respond in a particular way to a situation

**litter** group of newborn animals born to the same mother at the same time

**mammal** class of warmblooded animals that feed their young with milk from special mammary glands, have an internal backbone, and are more or less covered with hair

**medieval** period in European history from the 5th to about the 14th century AD

**moccasin** soft leather shoe first worn by Native American Indians

**mollusc** any member of a group of animals that have no backbone and are usually enclosed in a shell (for example, snails, clams, or squids)

**mussel** kind of mollusc (shellfish)

**muzzle** animal's snout (jaw and nose)

**nocturnal** active at night

**nostril** one of the outer openings of the nose

**oddity** unusual thing or quality

**parasite** creature that lives on another, which it usually injures

**plateau** wide land area with a fairly level surface raised sharply above the land on at least one side

**polio** serious disease that may kill or permanently weaken or paralyze its victims

**pollen** (verb: pollinate) very fine dusty substance that comes from flowers; it is important in reproduction of other plants

**polo** team sport played by hitting a wooden ball with mallets through goalposts while on horseback

**predator** (adjective: predatory) animal that lives by eating other animals

**prey** animal eaten by another animal

**primitive** ancient, or belonging to a very early stage of development

**prowl** creep about in a sneaky way, often while hunting

**pygmy** something very small for its kind

**rabies** serious disease of animals that is usually passed on through the bite of a sick (rabid) animal; its effects include extreme salivation, strange behaviour, and usually death

**reptile** major animal group that includes snakes, lizards, and other animals that usually have scales or bony plates

**research** careful search and study

**roam** to travel or wander freely through a wide area

**rodent** major animal group that includes mice, squirrels, and other small gnawing animals

**rudder** flat piece attached to the back of a boat or ship and used for steering

**sacred** holy

**Scandinavia** peninsula in northern Europe that includes the countries of Denmark, Norway, and Sweden

**sedge** plant group found in marshes and related to grasses and rushes

**semi-desert** area that is much like a desert but has more rainfall

**shears** cutting device similar to scissors but usually larger

**shortage** a situation of need, or an amount that is missing or isn't enough

**solitary** alone

**species** group of living things that have certain characteristics in common and share a name

**stationary** unmoving

**submerge** to put under water

**tapered** little by little becoming smaller toward one end

**temperament** personality or usual mood

**territorial** protective of a territory or home area

**tolerate** to put up with; also, to be able to survive

**tuft** short mound of fur

**tusk** long tooth that overhangs when the mouth is closed and serves for digging food or as a weapon

**vast** huge or spacious

**veterinarian** doctor who takes care of animals

**weaned** capable of and used to eating food rather than nursing